This Book Belongs to :

MW01433832

Printed by CreateSpace, An Amazon.com Company
A Publication by Nicole Planner

91568051R00057

Made in the USA
Middletown, DE
01 October 2018